MAKING
URBAN SCHOOLS
WORK

Social Realities
and the Urban School

MAKING URBAN SCHOOLS WORK

Social Realities and the Urban School

Mario Fantini
Program Officer
THE FORD FOUNDATION

Gerald Weinstein
UNIVERSITY OF MASSACHUSETTS

HOLT, RINEHART AND WINSTON, INC.
New York   Chicago   San Francisco   Atlanta   Dallas
Montreal   Toronto   London

FOREWORD

In one of his commentaries on revolutionary movements, Jean-Paul Sartre pointed out that in order to understand the struggles of men, we must first join in them. In a very real sense, this same advice holds today in the growing struggle to produce and promote a viable scheme of education for urban areas. This is, I hope, more than just another call for the academics to leave the ivory tower and go into the schools and communities of the urban ghetto; in this field at this time there are no invidious distinctions between the "firing line" and the drawing boards. In urban education, what is happening transcends the schools and involves the entire urban community. But after almost a decade of discussion and debate, we are still prescribing new combinations and recombinations of the same old nostrums for the ills of the city. What Mario Fantini and Gerald Weinstein have done in this little volume is to cast out the old prescriptions and ask in a refreshingly tentative way, "What is the best environment within which the urban child can learn and grow?" Ultimately, the case for successful urban education programs must rest on the proposition that they do make a difference in the lives of the children exposed to them. In fact, while the authors do not claim other than an urban context for their formulations, the ideas developed here have meaning for all educational programs regardless of their geographical setting. This volume is a first and significant step in conceptualizing a setting in which educational programs can be made to work.

May 1968

Francis A. J. Ianni
Director, Horace Mann—
Lincoln Institute
TEACHERS COLLEGE
COLUMBIA UNIVERSITY

PREFACE

Early this year we were asked by the Association for Supervision and Curriculum Development (ASCD) to prepare a paper on the "Urban School" for presentation in Atlantic City. Not many of us get a chance to construct a "dream" school; therefore we accepted the assignment with joy. Then came the frightening part! We all go through our professional lives as if we know what an ultimate educational system would look like, but when it comes time to "spell out" the details we realize how many gaps there are. In spite of these feelings we very quickly put together some of our thoughts within the guidelines of the questions: What is urban about urban schools? And, If we could create our own kind of urban school, what would it be like?

The response to our preliminary paper in Atlantic City encouraged us to expand the notions presented there. We wanted to expand them just enough to see how much interest we could generate and not so much that the reader would be swamped by the complexities that are bound to emerge. This book, then, represents the very beginnings, the mere skeletal outline of a model urban school. Our greatest hope is that some people will be inspired to begin working on the variety of tasks needed to create such an enterprise. We invite the reader to share in the specifications for programs and implementation, a task to which we will continue to devote much of our time and energy in the future years.

We should like to give special thanks to William Bristow and ASCD for getting us started; to Bruce Joyce at Teachers College, Columbia University, who provided us with the framework into which our curriculum notions could readily fit; to Diane Bassett Bertine for her unflagging editorial assistance; to Susan Burstein for typing the manuscript; and finally, to our publisher for allowing us to pursue this beginning venture.

New York   M.F.
May 1968   G.W.

CONTENTS

Foreword   *v*

Preface   *vii*

WHAT IS URBAN ABOUT AN URBAN SCHOOL?   *3*

   Density and Loss of Identity   *5*
   Bureaucratization and Powerlessness   *7*
   Diversity and Disconnectedness   *8*

GETTING SOCIAL REALITIES INTO THE SCHOOL   *11*

   Operational Constraints on Social Realities *11*
   Social Realities as a Means to Traditional Objectives *14*
   Social Realities and New Educational Objectives *16*

A MODEL OF AN URBAN SCHOOL   *24*

   The Objectives   *25*

School Organization Encompassing the Four Types
    of Objectives: The Three-Tiered School   30
Expanding the Notion of Tier III   33
Relationship of the Three-Tiered School
    to Society's Demands   40
Scheduling   44
Staffing   45
A Word About Teacher Training   50

RELATIONSHIP OF THE SCHOOL TO THE COMMUNITY   52

A Community School Serving People   52
Community Control and Urban Schools   55
Processes for Establishing a Tiered Urban School   57
Conclusion   61

MAKING URBAN SCHOOLS WORK

Social Realities and the Urban School

This book has three main purposes: to clarify what is distinctly urban about urban schools; to discuss how schools presently deal with the distinctions; and, finally, to suggest a way of making the distinctions more synonymous with a school's programming, staffing, and general organization. Before beginning to deal with these issues, however, we should like to mention the catalysts that prompt such a book.

We are living in a period of great social crisis—domestically and internationally—a crisis that is becoming increasingly difficult to ignore. It used to be that most of us were able to "tune out" rather easily whenever we were too depressed by the social dilemmas of our time. We knew there was segregation in the South, that there were lynchings now and then; and we were angry enough to contribute a few dollars to the National Association for the Advancement of Colored People (NAACP) and then sit back and forget about it. When it was pointed out that the North was racist too, it was accepted intellectually with an understanding nod, but we all knew that deep down it was the "average" white Southerner who was the real bigot. Those times of sloughing off the problem or blaming others for it seem to have gone forever. There are fewer and fewer places to hide as the blacks become more militant and demanding, and above all *violent*. Never before has it been so vehemently expressed to the white professional that he is incompetent and should therefore give up his authority because so many black children are failing in school. When in our past history has the white citizenry been told by so many that it is going to burn if it doesn't shape up?

What all this means is that we, the establishment, are becoming frightened. There is a persistent gnawing fear that our power is being gradually eroded and our competence undermined because basically it is being continually brought to our attention that our ways of going about things do not seem to work in the urban school, and more recently, even in the suburban school.[1] Somehow we are losing control over the situation. It seems to us that fear—perhaps with a good portion of helplessness mixed in—is a major catalyst effecting a consideration of the issues and problems of the urban school. It is our hope that some of these raw insistent feelings will allow us to face as directly as possible the dilemmas and somehow to create constructive, rather than defensive, responses.

If the problems of urban areas and urban schools are frightening to us, they are also mandating us to re-evaluate objectives, methodology, content, and virtually everything we know (or thought we knew) about education in general. Moreover, we are beginning to see that what is happening in large urban areas is really a preview of coming attractions for a major portion of our country. The concentration of problems we now view in stark bas relief in the urban schools is beginning to emerge, we believe, even in nonurban areas.

If this is so, what is it about the urban scene that is most pertinent to all of us and to education in general?

[1]See Alice Miel, *The Shortchanged Children of Suburbia.* Institute of Human Relations Press, The American Jewish Committee, New York, 1967, pamphlet series, no. 8.

WHAT IS URBAN ABOUT
AN URBAN SCHOOL?

If we were to choose the one characteristic of an urban context that has priority for schools it would be stated as follows:

The urban context is one in which *there is persistent stress imposed by intensely concentrated social realities*. Although all schools operate in a context of social realities, those that are in smaller more homogeneous communities have much less tension because the schools reflect a reality that is more parallel to that of the surrounding community. In addition, in those communities there is not the intense concentration of so many varied realities—so many different slices of life. The urban school, located in an area of great density and diversity, finds itself at a convergence point of a whole array of realities.

While most schools have devotedly divorced themselves from direct confrontations with social reality, the urban school stands out as most absurd in its emulation of the way reality is reflected in suburban schools. But, before we go into what the school is or is not doing, we must take a hard look at the urban social realities and the stress they impose.

Although there are numerous ways to describe and diagnose the persistent press of social realities in urban areas, time and space force us to limit this particular discussion. However, from reading what some of the "experts" in urban diagnosis have written and by using our own perceptions and experiences, we would like to single out those aspects that have a clearer (for us) relationship to educational prescriptions.

It will be necessary to describe briefly some of the concepts that shape our perceptions and help us diagnose the urban scene. Our general framework for examining the urban scene is this: How does the press of urban social realities affect certain basic human issues?

Human beings have a combination of personal issues with which they continually attempt to deal in some satisfactory manner. Many of these issues are common enough to be designated as a pattern— a "*human* issue." Although these human issues have been labeled through the years in a variety of different ways (needs, wants, concerns, drives, and so forth), all of these different labels have something in common.

These human issues can generally be grouped into issues revolving around safety, security, or survival, which include most of the physical needs—food, clothing, shelter, health—as well as the emotional needs for safety and security. A separate grouping can be made of those issues dealing with the psychosocial needs of love, recognition, status, affiliation and potency, agency or effect. In addition a third grouping may be made: one dealing with aesthetic, knowledge-seeking, spiritual, and self-actualizing issues. Once some of these issues are described, one can look at the cities with the question: What are the physical and psychosocial characteristics of city life and what effect do they have on its inhabitants in their attempts to work through the issues just described?

For the purpose of this writing we intend to deal with the middle range of issues described, the psychosocial group, and to limit even those to the issues of identity, connectedness or affiliation, and power (potency—agency—effect), and then to proceed to outline some of the effects of urban life on these issues.

By *identity* issues, we mean those aspects of a person's behavior which aim at providing him with a sense of worth. This area includes all the questions pertaining to the process of self-evaluation and the consequences of these evaluations. It is referred to by such terms as self-image, self-concept, identity, self-awareness, self-esteem, ego, ego-strength, and the like. All of these surround the basic questions: Who am I? What am I worth?

By *connectedness* issues we mean those aspects of a person's behavior which aim at providing him with a sense of positive affiliation with others. This is the relations-with-others domain, ranging from the primary face-to-face relations to secondary relations with less direct groups. Connectedness issues involve the questions: To whom does the individual feel an allegience? To whom does he feel he belongs? What are people to him? Who are the significant others? How does he relate? With whom does he *integrate?*

By *power* issues we mean those aspects of a person's behavior which aim at providing him with a sense of control or influence over what is happening and will happen to him. Does the individual feel that he has a significant part to play in the construction of situations that will affect him? If he does, does he act in accordance with these feelings?

Although these issues are usually integrated and less distinct as discrete personal arenas in individuals, we think it is helpful to keep them separate as we now examine some of the social realities of the urban context and their relation to these issues.

Density and Loss of Identity

To what extent do the urban realities contribute to the identity crisis of the city dweller. Do I really count? Do I have any importance? Am I being lost in the massive shuffle of the big city life? These are often the unverbalized questions of the city dwellers—all of which may be condensed into: How does the city affect my perceptions of myself?

Everyone knows that cities are crowded, that space is at a premium, that it is difficult to get away from crowds of hustling, bustling people. Everywhere there are lines of people waiting. Subway trains provide for some of the most physically intimate rides obtainable anywhere. But what is the persistent stress on the individual confronted with great numbers of people? We would contend that the result is greater depersonalization, less empathy, greater feelings of loneliness and anonymity, and a general hardening or mechanization of relationships with people.

Varied comments of urban dwellers reflect this description:

> I don't feel sorry for nobody. When you been around this town as long as I've been and ya seen all the nuts and kooks, it just runs off your back like water.

> How can I possibly count as anything important when I've never felt more lonely in my life than when I moved to the city? Everyone seems to be in such a hurry to get to his own hidden little world. Strange to feel so lonely when there are so many people around.

People living in extremely close physical contact with one another and highly dependent, yet remaining isolated in general from one another—a sea of unknown faces—is just one of the paradoxes of the urban social reality of size and density. Impersonal relationships are numerous here, and the brief casual contacts between persons allow in most instances for the communication of only superficial information. Yet, on the basis of this limited information, people evaluate and rank others. Standardized, superficial criteria for stratifying people thus evolve according to address, speech, manners, skin color, dress, and so forth.[2] There are too many people to absorb as individuals; therefore, a categorical depersonalized shorthand becomes reinforced.

Within the urban school itself, depersonalization is dramatically evident. Class size has rarely been pared down, in spite of "average" numbers issued in board of education reports. Having *every* child study the same thing at the same time for the same length of time is the rule. Teachers rarely live in the same community in which they teach, and thus parents and teachers are strangers. Because of the great numbers of children, cumulative records and reports in effect become the "children" about whom standardized decisions are made.

[2]See James M. Beshar, *Urban Social Structure.* New York: The Free Press, 1962, p. 46.

Personalizing education would mean fouling up the machinery of the organization and by all means the machinery comes before the individual or else we would have chaos.

This problem of depersonalization brings us to our next major social reality of the urban area.

Bureaucratization and Powerlessness

In spite of Mayor Lindsay's pronouncement that New York City shall be known as Fun City, living there has been like being a member of "Strike-of-the-Month-Club." In the last three years the city has had subway, newspaper, hospital workers', teachers', garage, taxicab, and, most recently, garbage workers' strikes. Many of these caused considerable inconvenience to the urban residents. What struck us, the authors, however, was the degree of nonchalance with which the citizens endured these events with an "Oh, well, it will be over soon" attitude. It was almost as if people were being reminded that this was the price they had to pay for living in Fun City—or for that matter, in any large city. James Reston, in an editorial in *The New York Times,* was astounded at the complacent and passive reaction of the New York citizenry. "The force [the bureaucracy] is so powerful," he writes, "that they are beyond reason or persuasion or control. Power will tell in the end, they seem to be saying, and the people are merely spectators and victims in the struggle."[3] "You can't fight City Hall" is the dominant theme. The bigger the city, the less feeling of control, so why bother?

Anyone who has gone through the experience of trying to get help on a problem from a large city agency and of then being passed from one official to another has an emotional sense of the castrating effect of such an experience. The public is regarded by frustrated bureaucratic clerks as an imposition, an obstacle, a digression from their work, which is, ironically, to serve the public.

And so it happens within the urban school, as indicated in this vignette observed by the authors:

[3]"New York; The City That Quit," editorial by James Reston, *The New York Times,* October 22, 1965.

SCENE: An urban elementary school; outside the main office
TIME: First day of school; registration
CHARACTERS: School secretary and about twenty mothers and their children
PROPS: None; no chairs, nothing, just a wall and a floor
SECRETARY: *(Shouting)* Will you ladies line up against that wall please—we'll be with you as soon as we can! *(disappears into office. One hour passes. Children are restless and noisy. Mothers are reprimanding the children.)*
SECRETARY: *(Shouting)* Will you please keep those kids quiet. Can't you see how busy we are! *(Disappears into office. Mothers and children still kept waiting uncomfortably; a feeling of their insignificance in terms of the operation of the school sets in.)*

Many people question public institutions as to who serves whom. The verdict rendered most often is that in reality the client is at the service of the institution. Thus "You can't fight City Hall" has become "You can't fight the Board of Education." As cogs in a gigantic machinery, administrators, teachers, children, and parents are rendered powerless in persistent ways.

The following statements help to sum up this powerlessness vis-à-vis bureaucracy and urban living: "For satisfaction and growth, people need to engage in active interchange with their environment; to use it, organize it, even destroy it. . .[their] physical surroundings [and institutions][4] should be accessible and open-ended. . ."[5] The present urban social reality is very far from this ideal.

Diversity and Disconnectedness

To what extent does the city create a context for connectedness between different people? Does it engender a sense of community in which its variety of people see each other as important and related to one another? Does it create a sense of belonging?

Of all the social realities faced by the urban dwellers and especially the urban school, the tremendous diversity of people looms as the

[4]Authors' insertion.
[5]From the chapter by Kevin Lynch, "The city as environment" in *Cities*. (A Scientific American Book.) New York: Knopf-Random House, 1966, p. 194.

most crucial distinction. Because so many different kinds of people, attitudes, perceptions, values, and habits are concentrated in a limited geographical area, this may be cited as one of the most unique aspects of an urban environment.

It is one thing, however, to know that diversity is a fact of urban life; it is quite another to realize how diversity is viewed by the urban resident. To a few, diversity provides an exciting possibility for enrichment and expansion of one's own perceptions and experiences through a kind of cross-fertilizing interaction between different groups of people. These are the few who thrive on variety and find it nourishing. But we think that this attitude is not the one prevalent in the city. More often diversity is viewed as threatening, and at best as novel or interesting but certainly not anything one would consciously seek to develop. It is in the city, typically, that the great potential for cross-fertilization lies and yet the distinct ethnic and racial turfs are entered by others only when absolutely necessary. It seems as if the only meeting ground between these diverse groups is in the restaurant—but then only recipes and foods cross-fertilize, not the people. Physical and psychological boundaries that keep people disconnected and alienated from one another are as well maintained as the Berlin Wall.

The urban school, meanwhile, has always considered itself the great homogenizer. It has taken great masses of diverse people and acculturated them to the middle-class mainstream. Whether or not specifically articulated as such, this is what the mission of the school was and is. Only *now* something seems to be going wrong. The acculturation mission is having tremendous bumps and wobbles. Many of the processes established by the school are intended to stamp out diversity, both cultural and individual, so that the urban school actually alienates diverse pupils and keeps them disconnected from the school. Until recently, for example, it was illegal in New York for a teacher in a school to speak in Spanish to Spanish-speaking pupils except in foreign language classes.

If we now go back to our initial characterization of the urban milieu—which was stated as "the persistent stress imposed by intensely concentrated social realities"—we can summarize in this way: density and size, bureaucracy, and diversity are social realities which persistently lay stress on the individual's concern for identity, power, and connectedness. Certainly there are other ways to select and categorize social realities; however, we think this will serve our present purposes.

The stresses we have been discussing also imply that a city dweller has less opportunity to ignore social realities. He is exposed to them whether he wants to be or not. He is close to crime, riots, poverty, muggings, alcoholics—they are constantly making themselves felt—and he cannot remain totally impervious to them. So it is with children in the urban school: The urban school has attempted to shy away from things going on in the real world which are part of an urban child's experience. Thus there is dichotomy and tension between the child's urban curriculum and the school's more antiseptic curriculum—a dichotomy that usually leads the urban child to label the school's curriculum as "phony."

We have been saving a final descriptive characterization for last in order to emphasize it. What we have been discussing up to now are some of the effects of urbanization on the "average" resident—who could very well be middle-class and white. Depersonalization, anonymity, isolation, powerlessness, can be and *are* felt by people whose bellies are relatively full, who have steady incomes, and who have not been discriminated against by society. Now, however, it is becoming more evident that increasingly the "average" city dweller is more likely to be poor and discriminated against. Public schools in large cities are basically the habitat of the socioeconomically disadvantaged and will become more so. Therefore if the characteristics of urban stress are felt by those who are relatively well-off, we must magnify those stresses, perhaps double or triple them, when applying them to the disadvantaged resident. We must also magnify those stresses when applying them to the urban public school itself. The urban school thus finds itself in the center of a situation where the black demands for power, identity, and connectedness are hammering on its doors with ever-increasing insistence.

GETTING SOCIAL REALITIES INTO THE SCHOOL

Operational Constraints on Social Realities

Thus far we have sketched certain social realities that surround urban schools and the psychosocial concerns so closely related to these realities. The question now becomes: What role should the urban school assume vis-à-vis the social realities and concerns? That the urban school should play a role has already been assumed, for if the urban school (or any school, for that matter) declares no role, then it would admit to dealing with *social unreality*—a pedagogically unjustifiable position. Or the school must make the case that the content and process of the standard school already deals with social realities— a case that would be spotty at best.

In order for the urban school to deal with these social realities in an authentic, direct way, certain *operational* (actual) pedagogical realities must be identified and analyzed to determine their influence on the urban school's capacity for dealing with social reality.

Let us begin with the operational definition of *quality education* which is the day-to-day yardstick used for assessing a good school by the interested parties involved with public education: parents, communities, teachers, administration, school boards, state departments of education, teachers' organizations, and so forth. Stated simply, the operational definition is "grade level or above performance in basic skills and academic achievement, as measured by standardized tests" (for example, the Iowa Basic Skills, Regents Examinations, and so forth). Ghetto parents want their children to be reading at grade level, not two or three years behind; suburban, economically advantaged parents want their children to be two or three years above grade level in reading, and so forth. Grade level achievement takes on increased importance to the interested parties also because college entry is dependent on adequate achievement in these same academic skill areas. Consequently the mission of the school has been forged, and a structure (for example, bureaucracy, a graded system, and so on) and a process from early childhood to college has been formulated to meet the mission.

This concensus on what "quality education" is, on what schools are for, can be challenged or disturbed only at the risk of persistent retaliation by the interested publics. We are all familiar with the term "frill" which is attached to any attempt to introduce into the standard educational process any "alien" content—even if it be content that deals with such fundamental issues as alienation, identity, power, connectedness, talent, career, or the like. Consequently social reality of the types depicted earlier cannot be introduced into the present urban school without bumping directly into the operational definition of quality education. Such social realities of necessity must be made *relevant* to this operational definition if their entry into the institution is to be initiated. The onus of responsibility is therefore on those who seek more social reality in the school; it is their task to justify its relationship to "quality education."

For some seeking to deal with the social reality of cultural identity for black people, the introduction of Swahili into the school may be attempted, only to find the verdict that Swahili is irrelevant to the present definition of quality education. Yet Swahili has been included as an "elective" in certain urban schools, thereby giving us an idea that the school may consider "adding" or building appendages in for certain social realities. But the bulk of the content of social reality stands apart, waiting to be legitimized by the urban school and hitting head on with the institutional constraints that restrict fundamental tampering with the traditional content. "Covering" the year's worth of current academic content remains a gatekeeper of the present system and is to all intents and purposes the primary objective of urban education.

To pursue the pervasive effects on the institution of the operational definition of "quality education" let us analyze its effect on the professional. For example, the teacher, the institutional agent closest to the learner, is imprisoned by this definition. On one hand, the urban teacher admits that the children are not responding to the standard education content and approaches and admits that new content and testing strategies are desperately needed. On the other hand, he is constrained by the accepted institutional norms regulating pedagogic behavior ("Don't be a rebel," "Play the game") and by a form of organization which isolates him from his colleagues. The result is that teachers and administrators develop mechanisms to cope with the "institutional realities." Teachers argue that given the existing system, "quality education" could be purveyed by them if five conditions were met:

1. Smaller classes
2. Riddance of disruptive children who disturb the class
3. Materials that keep learners engaged
4. Freedom from routine administrative details and interruptions
5. Higher salaries

These demands by teachers are quite realistic given the institutional setting in which they are asked to implement "quality" education; even though, thus far, where these conditions have been implemented, the results still are not encouraging.

The point is that an entire formal school process and organization (for example, school design, staff utilization, teacher certifications, and the like) has been structured to deal with a traditional and, to us, outdated definition of quality education. Despite changes in the assignment that society has given to the school in recent years, (for example, the growing demands that the school give education for diversity, for *all,* and for the social roles that are needed in our society), the old ways prevail. Those in the educational institution charged with the responsibility for realizing quality education as well as those outside the system (each of whom is the product of the standard educational process) hold to the conventional wisdom—to the conventional definition of quality education. Therefore, it seems that the major road open for bringing social realities into existing urban schools would be to stress the relevance of social realities for improving basic skills and standard academic achievement. If this were done, however, social realities would become, at best, new means to old ends.

Social Realities as a Means to Traditional Objectives

Despite the fact that the use of social realities for improving standard academic achievement is really only a way of getting learners to old ends, let us examine how this might be done. Social realities can be legitimized in the institution and can foster traditional educational objectives in several ways.

The present social studies curriculum and curriculums in the other disciplines in urban elementary schools can be expanded to include units on varied social realities. Thus, the unit on the American Indians could include a section on the plight of modern Indians, enriched possibly by poignant samples of the songs of modern folk singers such as Buffy St. Marie; the unit on the American Negro could deal with the poverty of current ghetto existence; the unit on understanding other cultures could include at least the fact that three quarters of the world is starving; and so on. Secondary urban schools might develop a new course entitled "Urban Social Realities," in which many of the problems identified earlier in this paper could be covered. Teacher-training institutions could add a course for prospective teachers, called "Teaching Social Realities to Urban Youth." The creative teacher could augment any of these units or courses by readings in sociology on the urban milieu (including news clippings on the recent Riot Commission's report); by field trips to ghetto areas;

by films on tenement living or the aftermath of summer riots; or by guest speakers who have worked with addicts, dropouts, and similar people.

The children exposed to these "new" areas would, we suspect, proceed to write about them and be marked for originality, grammar, punctuation, spelling, and the like. These "new" experiences could become the basis for experience stories to increase interest in reading for minority children. Of course, some discussion on the implications of the social realities on human beings in general and on the learner himself may be expected to emerge. If these dialogues develop, however, the likelihood is great that the discussion will deal with diagnoses and sharpened descriptions of the social reality problem. If students begin to ask what they personally should *do* about the problem and decide upon forming a protest group and marching on the local political leader, the teacher would probably try to discourage such prescriptions (partly because of his own image and welfare, given the present "ground rules" of acceptable behavior governing the professional teacher in the big city school systems).

Although we have been perhaps overly facetious in the preceding paragraphs about slipping the social realities in as a means to traditional ends, let us state sincerely that if social realities entered the school program even as a means only for making contact with the learner and for taking him toward the basic skills and academic objectives presently emphasized, the present school program would, we feel, be greatly enriched. Moreover, we must once again underscore that we are not for one moment suggesting the abandonment of basic skills or academic mastery; on the contrary, we propose to argue their importance and continuation. Our concern is that they have become *all*-important and that all new content is legitimized mainly as a vehicle to be manipulated toward the academic objectives, thus attributing a second class status to content such as social reality. We propose to argue later that basic skills and academic mastery could be dealt with more efficiently if the urban school were organized differently. We also propose to offer a different interpretation for defining what is relevant to the needs of both society and the learner in urban schools.

Our fear is that if social realities were to be used exclusively as a basic pedagogic strategy for getting learners to perform better in traditional skill areas, it would do a basic injustice to both the social realities and the skill areas. We believe that the learner would sense a "phoniness" about this strategy and that such a feeling would dilute the potential learning inherent in a curriculum of social reality. For example, if the black student senses that the inclusion of "black power" in the social studies program really is being used to lead him toward other "irrelevant" academic mastery he may retreat from involvement with both areas.

What we see then as the most beneficial way of introducing social realities into the school is to stress social realities as content in their own right—content that has intrinsic value because it is integrally related to the learner, to his personal concerns, and to the needs of an open, self-renewing society.

Social Realities
and New Educational Objectives

Social Action

What we are suggesting is that social realities can become important content for *making contact* with, and maintaining the sustained involvement of, diverse urban student populations.[6] The very nature of social realities can at least engage the learner temporarily, either because of the deviation perceived by students from the rather antiseptic curriculum of present-day schooling or because social realities contain the seeds of an intrinsic relevance to the learners' basic concerns. This phase we label "making contact."

The tricky part is what happens after contact. If schools go from contact mainly toward the traditional academic areas, we have been suggesting that the contact will not last and that kids will not play the game because the traditional academic content is irrelevant to many. This does *not* mean that social reality has no role in increasing

---

[6]For a fuller explanation of the *contact* approach, see "Toward a Relevant Curriculum" *in* Mario D. Fantini and Gerald Weinstein, *The Disadvantaged: Challenge to Education.* New York: Harper & Row, 1968, p. 337.

academic performance. We simply are making the point that to *overload* social realities for this purpose would be a less viable strategy than to explore new learning objectives—objectives that, ironically, would coincide with what educators and political statesmen have been proclaiming for *centuries* to be the legitimate responsibilities of public schools as major social institutions. Those responsibilities or, as they are often called, "broad aims" of education are namely to foster in all learners those behaviors that lead to genuine concern for—and action upon—creating environments that favorably effect the development of individual human potential. The new specific objectives should lead to the more humanistically oriented goals of an open society. In short, the school should develop in each learner, behavior more consonant with participatory democracy.

This is a tall order and quite a leap for the urban schools to take at this time, for several very real reasons. First, as we have indicated, the dominance of academic mastery objectives sharply limits the achievement of other types of objectives especially when children in urban schools are performing so poorly in these very basic areas. Second, the school organization is not geared to serve adequately other objectives. Third, and perhaps most important, if social realities are introduced as a means for developing learners who practice participatory democracy, the consequences of this participation could be quite controversial. Regarding this third point, one needs only mention the reactions to the recent organized student protests and marches in various urban schools. To utilize social realities, then, as a means for achieving new educational objectives aimed at helping an individual *act upon* the social realities, must be thought through quite carefully. If we do not approach this area systematically, the consequences may not only jeopardize the inclusion of social realities into the educational process, but may also result in heightened frustrations of the learners themselves and of the other parties who make up public education.

Perhaps, in order to approach this systematically, we must take into consideration the various levels to which social reality objectives should be aimed. Assuming people want new objectives that are more intrinsically related to social realities, there are a number of levels in which even these can be approached.

At first, the new objectives might be directed only at making contact with the learners and making them more aware of the social realities. Assuming that contact is made with the learners, however, the next question is: After contact, what? What would be the next phase or level of approaching the new objectives?

The second level appears to be awareness in more personal terms. That is, objectives could be developed which would help the learner begin to understand not only the nature and implication of the social realities discussed and analyzed, but also that *he* is a part of the very social reality being assessed. For example, the learner exposed to the higher disease rate for ghetto dwellers may not only understand this as a fact, but may even begin to link the implication to his own welfare or to that of his friends, family, community, or nation. If the linkage to his own intrinsic concern is made, the result may be increased anxiety or fear that is either suppressed or overt. The questions now become: What does the school offer the learner at this point? What tools would the school have ready for the learner to deal with his own anger? Does the present orientation of the teacher, counselor, school psychologist, or administrator provide for the proper handling of such hostility?

Ironically, many urban learners are being taught by other teachers in the hidden curriculum that exists outside the school, such as community leaders who can articulate the plight of the poor, of the black people, of minorities who are being victimized by an apathetic white society. The learners' frustration, anger, and hostility at the realization that they have been victims of a negative environment, triggers emotional energies which are not being constructively dealt with, either outside or inside the urban school.

Once social realities become linked to the learners' own existence (for example, feelings such as "My chances of getting a good paying job in a white racist society are limited," or, "When I'm out of my neighborhood I feel like a fish out of water"), awareness takes on a different character. When, further, the learner becomes aware that most slums can be eliminated if certain priorities are established by the city, state, or nation, then the awareness becomes connected to questions about who should be doing what about it?

The learner may then take the step from exposure to the social realities of, for instance, slum life to the broader conceptual generalization that environments shape growth and development for each person either negatively or positively and that if the learner, as an individual, is in what can be assessed to be a negative environment, then that same environment is thwarting his human potential and life chance.

Once at this stage we suggest that the learner may take a step further. He may begin to think that his options, given his understanding of the generalization, are to:

1. Learn to *cope* or *adjust* to the negative environment (for example, a ghetto)
2. Learn how to get out into a positive environment
3. Learn how to fight blindly in the negative environment
4. Learn the strategies and systems for reconstructing the negative environment.

When the learner reaches this stage, he is beyond simple awareness and is thinking about actual options or alternatives for action.

At this point even though the learner has used social realities as a tool for serious thought and feeling and for considering alternative actions, no *direct action* need follow. For example, even though the learner may be aware that his chances of "making it" (succeeding) are limited, he may not be motivated to the point of taking action, or he may lack the know-how for taking such action. We believe that both cognitive and affective (that is, an emotional bond, linking the social realities to his own intrinsic concerns) connections are necessary in order to move the learner closer to the level of direct action and participation and to begin to deal with deeper questions of identity and connectedness.

However, a third level is also necessary—role behavior, or the *performing, doing, acting* level. Thinking and, later, feeling behavior has characterized the earlier stages of awareness; but it is not enough to think about the social realities problems. At some point personal action must follow thought. A learner can think (and probably feel strongly) about the negative environment that has been affecting his life for years, but until he acts as an agent to reconstruct the environment, the cycle to true participatory democracy will not have been completed. This stage requires *clinical* opportunities for learners to behave in adult *role* situations. The role of participant will develop when the learner is placed in reality contexts in which he can actively perform his role directly. This may run the range from the simple writing of letters to political leaders, to marching on city hall, to working in preschool centers, to involvement in community-action projects, or in domestic peace corps programs or international Peace Corps programs. Thus a new set of objectives related to social realities must be formulated to help the learner deal with this action level.

If the school intends to consider objectives other than those geared to academic mastery, rather profound changes in schooling have to be made. Objectives related to social participation and personal development cannot be left to chance. The consequences on the individual, the public school, and society are too great. Moreover, it must be remembered that it is not a matter of substituting social realities for academic skills, but rather of creating a setting in which *all* these objectives can be realized.

The Self

Before we suggest an actual model for an urban school that is organized to deal with these next sets of educational objectives, we have to emphasize that a set of objectives related to individual identity problems must be developed. During our exposition of participation we touched on the related problem confronting all urban youth—the social reality of *self*. The urban learner joins all others in asking the fundamental question: Who am I?

Lately in educational circles especially, the term "self concept" has occupied more discussion time than ever before. However, like the weather, everyone talks about it but very little is done about it. A number of well-done studies and summaries focusing on Negro self concept have been made, but as usual the present structure permits very limited prescription based on these studies. Within the confines of the academic objectives of schools, however, some attempts have been made to do something about self concept.

The very first set of prescriptions that schools attempted was the use of "role-models." All we have to do is parade a host of successful black people before the pupils so that they can see that it is possible to "make it" in this society. Thus, in many assembly programs around the country black doctors, lawyers, engineers, and other professionals were asked to speak to the pupils on the value of education. In some instances this had an effect, but in others the pupils could not have cared less. These role-models were not the pupils' heroes but were those who the white establishment thought these kids should have as their heroes. The heroes of the pupils were more action-oriented; they were athletes and entertainers—but no one wished to reinforce the stereotype of the only successful Negroes being in sports and entertainment. Now, incidently, new heroes are emerging in the ghettos: the black militants who are actively engaged in a battle with the white power structure. We wonder if these new heroes will be involved in present and future assembly programs.

A second popular mode for hitting the self-concept issue was through the organization of the subject matter. The hypothesis was, and still is, that the more success experiences the children have in school, the more their self concepts will improve. Thus, if we organize what we are teaching into smaller steps and provide immediate reinforcement, the child will succeed more often and gain a feeling of mastery over the subject matter with the result that his self concept will be enhanced through his competency in academic achievement.

Again, if this were done it would represent a great improvement over what currently exists in urban schools. However, its payoff to improve self concept is limited, we feel, to that area in which the competency is being demonstrated. Certainly it is a great feeling when one finally feels he is able to read or to compute accurately or to figure out a science problem: it provides a sense of potency within the social system of the school, but the transfer potential of feelings of competency and self-worth in math to a complicated "real life" situation where the press on self-worth is really intense is rather slight. We may all feel fairly competent professionally—but how is it when we go home?

Another popular mode for dealing with self concept is through the introduction of Afro-American history into the curriculum. If black children especially could see more of their own cultural roots and what happened to them in this country, if they could see how the black man played a vital role in the development of this country, then perhaps they would acquire a greater sense of dignity in themselves and in their people. Also, if this knowledge were not relegated to only one week out of the year but instead were part of the everyday curriculum, it would have a more definite and pervasive impact on the children. Again, we encourage this approach not only for black schools but for *all* schools.

Nevertheless, there are still some nagging problems. Very few children enjoy studying history that much—be it their own or anybody else's. A good teacher can make it come alive, of course; but there are not that many good teachers. Furthermore, much of the 300-year history of the Negroes in the United States involves the story of their horrible containment by this country. How can the truth be presented so that it does not reinforce negative images on the part of the Negro youngster? Black militants are saying that it is because the history has been written by whites that there is danger of negative reinforcement. And that very possibly is true. This must be a consideration if the introduction of Afro-American history is going to enhance self concept.

Finally, the most popular mode of intervention to affect self concept is aimed at the teacher-pupil interaction system. If we can get teachers to improve their "attitudes" toward the youngsters so as to create an atmosphere and relationships that are more accepting, understanding and open, the child's self concept will be enhanced. Fine —we want this very much—we would like all teachers to be able to do this, but it is difficult. We know of some who have done it, but when the child leaves that teacher and goes to one more ordinary, what does the pupil retain that he can use in this situation and that does not depend on the presence of his former teacher?

These four intervening modes are really about the best that can be formulated given the academic performance objectives. All were created to fit somehow into the established structure without interfering too much with its basic process.

What would happen, however, if instead of using only the above modes of intervention, the school considered a set of objectives, and a curriculum supporting those objectives, that would allow for a direct engagement on the part of the learner with the issue of self concept or self-conceptualizing? That is, what would happen if the schools considered an organized approach to help learners work through their own self-perceiving processes? More will be said about the specifies of such objectives later.

Thus, while participatory democracy is needed (the social reconstruction role does help create feelings of individual and group potency), the process does not automatically deal with the inner reconstruction of the individual. Objectives must also be devised that focus on the inner world of the learner, on new ways for him to negotiate with himself and cope with his basic sense of connectedness or disconnectedness with others.

A MODEL OF AN
URBAN SCHOOL

After all this description of urban realities and analysis of their effects, what kind of prescription for the urban school is possible? According to the diagnosis given thus far, we shall offer a suggestion for a beginning model of an urban school that is directly connected with the issues we have raised. Therefore, corresponding to the limits we have given ourselves, the model would have to meet the following criteria:

1. Social reality and the school's curriculum have to be intrinsically connected.
   a. The school must acknowledge the realities by setting up a structure in which children are engaged in the examination of these realities.
   b. Children will learn the skills and behaviors needed to influence social realities.
   c. The skills and behaviors for social change will be applied by the children to the social realities.

2. Power, identity, and connectedness have to become a legitimized basis for curriculum development with the aim of expanding the repertoire of responses children have in dealing with these concerns.

3. Diversity, both cultural and individual, and its potential for cross-fertilization has to be encouraged and expanded through educational objectives and organization that allow and legitimize such an aim.

4. The school and the community it serves have to exist less as separate entities and instead develop responsibilities and lines of authority that are more integrated and shared.

Our construction of the model will have four major directions: (1) to consider an expansion and change in form of educational objectives; (2) to chart succinctly what a school that follows through on these objectives would look like organizationally; (3) to explore more fully some of the unique aspects of such a school; (4) to consider the relationship of this school to what society demands. In addition, after constructing the model we will address ourselves briefly to the questions of scheduling, staffing, and teacher training.

The Objectives

"A" Objectives

For a starter we can begin with four kinds of objectives, only one set of which is presently legitimized in the schools.

The legitimate ones ("A" objectives), as we have repeatedly indicated, are those that are geared to the attainment of academic skills and subject matter content. These are the objectives that rule the educational roost (in spite of the fact that they have not succeeded in achieving many of our broader educational aims). These are the objectives that almost all educational "innovations" are tuned into. When these are the sole objectives of education all descriptions and diagnoses of any group of people or of any area (for example, urban) become very difficult, because they must be squeezed into subject-matter goals. If we discuss power, identity, diversity, connectedness, and all the other issues we have mentioned, it becomes quite a challenge to try to fit those issues into teaching tasks that have as their aims getting children:

1. To read, to compute, to outline
2. To know the causes of the Civil War
3. To become familiar with the geography of Latin America
4. To know the parts of speech
5. To know the material that constitutes the Earth's crust

We certainly do not intend to deny the value of such tool skills and knowledge, but we find it difficult to relate sociopsychological descriptions to such objectives. In fact, we think this is a major reason for so many urban teachers becoming annoyed with consultants and with special resource people who feed teachers descriptions and analyses of their pupils. For they, the teachers, are constantly being put in the position of implementing a description when none of their teaching tasks have any intrinsic relation to those descriptions.

We have consistently had our knuckles rapped for the off-handed way we treat "A" objectives. However, we did not care much, because the objectives we were most interested in have been, and still are, treated in an off-handed way by those in the educational power structure. It was not until we were reprimanded by our colleague Bruce Joyce that we began to reconsider. Joyce, in his book *Alternative Models for Education,* has cogently spread out a menu of academic strategies from which objectives might be derived.[7] He lists as educational strategies those that deal with:

1. Symbolic-technical proficiency (reading, arithmetic, and so forth)
2. Information from selected disciplines (commonly, history and geography)
3. Structure of knowledge (concepts from disciplines)
4. Modes of inquiry (how scholars think)
5. Broad philosophical schools or problems (aesthetics, ethics, and so on)

---

[7]Bruce Joyce, *Alternative Models for Education.* Waltham, Mass.: Blaisdell Publishing Company, to be publ. fall, 1968.

It is fairly clear to us that, in reality, schools concern themselves largely with Strategies 1 and 2, "Symbolic-technical proficiency" and "Information from selected disciplines." Given *only* these two strategies, we can reiterate our frustration in trying to relate sociopsychological description to them. However, using a combination of the last three strategies on the list makes it easier to relate them to our diagnosis. If we use Strategies 3 through 5 in order to develop academic objectives we would begin by raising such questions as:

a. What *concepts* from what disciplines, or what *philosophical schools of thought* have the greatest priority for the urban issues as we have defined them?

or

b. What *modes of inquiry* from what kinds of scholars would have the greatest priority?

Thus, while still acknowledging the importance of and including skills and subject achievement objectives as a portion of the schools' responsibility, we would like to suggest three more sets of objectives:

"B" Objectives

1. To have the children acquire the skills of negotiating with adults
2. To have the children devise a variety of strategies for getting something they want
3. To have the children learn to identify the real power sources in their community
4. To have the children develop the skills of organizing people in order to create some change in their immediate social realities
5. To have the children learn to use all forms of media in order to gain support for some social action they intend to take
6. To have the children develop general skills for constructive social action such as[8]

---

[8] These are basically problem-solving and scientific method skills, but here they are applied directly to social action.

a. The ability to define clearly the objectives of social action

b. The ability to evaluate the existing situation, to identify obstacles to the goal, and to identify the available resources for overcoming these obstacles

c. The ability to analyze and to generate alternative measures for action, and to predict the various outcomes of each alternative

d. The ability to select the most valuable of these alternatives and to test them through action

e. The ability to evaluate the tested procedure and to revise strategies, thus beginning the cycle again[9]

If curriculums were developed with these types of objectives as their focus, we would begin to see a more intrinsic linkage between a teaching task and descriptions of powerlessness.

"C" Objectives

1. To have the children become aware of how whom they live with and where they live influence how they perceive themselves
2. To have the children learn how society's definitions of groups of people affect the way they judge themselves
3. To have the children analyze the criteria they are using for self-judgment in terms of its objective base
4. To have the children become more capable of predicting their own behavior
5. To have the children expand their repertoire of responses to situations
6. To have the children see themselves as more differentiated "subselves"[10]

---

[9]Fantini and Weinstein, *The Disadvantaged: Challenge to Education*, p. 436.

[10]Briefly, a subself may be thought of as one of the many characters of the self, each of which plays different roles and whose interaction with one another constitutes a unified self-image. Sample characters or subself voices heard during a specific situation might be: (1) the critic subself, (2) the loving subself, (3) the hurt, sorrowful child subself, (4) the protecting subself, (5) the observing subself. The concept of subselves is derived from Dr. Stewart Shapiro, whose article "Transactional Aspects of Ego Therapy," *The Journal of Psychology* (1963), pp. 487–489, explains the term more fully.

7. To have the children discover strengths, talents, and interests within themselves of which they may not now be aware

Although these objectives are crudely stated, we hope that one can begin to see their relationship with the descriptions of the urban dweller's concern for identity.

"D" Objectives

1. To expand the child's repertoire for interaction with others
2. To expand the child's repertoire for interaction with more kinds of others
3. To expand one's capacity for self-disclosure to others
4. To expand one's capacity for taking the risks in going out to others unilaterally
5. To expand one's circle of significant identifications
6. To expand one's ability to "experience other people as they really are, *i.e.,* to become able to really listen, to really develop a kind of third ear for the music that he's playing as well as the particular notes and words—what he's trying to say as well as what he is actually saying in words"[11]

One can begin to see the relationship between "D" objectives and a concern for connectedness. Moreover, this set of objectives is particularly poignant in a society that has been diagnosed as "white racist" by the President's Commission on Civil Disorders.[12]

When one thinks of all of the energy that has gone into the curriculum reform movement without even considering curriculum that might achieve the types of objectives listed in these last three categories, one begins to wonder if we are really serious about dealing with the basic concerns of our society.

[11]Abraham H. Maslow, *Eupsychian Management.* Homewood, Ill.: Richard D. Irwin, Inc., and the Dorsey Press, 1965, p. 168.
[12]*Report of the National Advisory Commission on Civil Disorders.* New York: Bantam Books, Inc., March 1968.

School Organization Encompassing the Four Types of Objectives: The Three-Tiered School[13]

In visualizing a school that facilitates the attainment of these objectives, picture a school that has the following three distinctive missions or areas of responsibility (a three-tiered school):

I. Skills and knowledge development
II. Personal talent and interest-identification and development
III. Social action and explorations of self and others

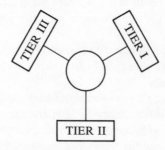

FIGURE 1   The three-tiered school

Tier I is comprised of objectives related to basic skills, learning to learn skills,[14] information, and the major concepts of specific disci-

---

[13]The three-tiered model was suggested to us by Bruce Joyce in the publication *Restructuring Elementary Education: A Multiple Learnings Systems Approach.* New York: Teachers College, Columbia University, 1966, p. 4.

[14]Learning to learn skills refers to those processes, ways of thinking, examining, or behaving which help the child become more adept at learning and which have been described by many educators as: critical thinking, analytic procedures, discussions procedures, rational processes, inquiry, evaluating, problem solving, hypothesizing, planning, predicting outcomes, generating alternatives, classification, analogy, comparison, inductive and deductive reasoning, and the like. The point to be made here, however, is that we do not regard these process skills as an outcome or end product in themselves. Although such skills may be more or less handled in rudimentary ways in Tier I, it is in Tiers II and III that we hope they will be exercised to the fullest. For instance, many people believe that if a child can be instructed in critical thinking that is all he needs. As important as critical thinking and other process skills are for the learner, we feel that they should be a means, an instrumentality, for helping children handle things that they are concerned about intrinsically. Thus, while introduced in Tier I, process skills will be utilized more meaningfully in Tiers II and III.

plines that are most needed as essential building blocks for the cognitive development of the child. Tier I thus includes reading, computation, writing, and speaking skills and the basic information and ideas contained in the social studies, science, and other disciplines. We would also include here ideas from psychology, sociology, anthropology, and political science and would substitute these ideas and concepts for much of what is currently taught in social studies, English, and science. It is important to note that any of this substitution should be weighed against the ultimate mission of the school. That is, given what we have in Tier I, which of it has the greatest priority for serving the concerns of connectedness, identity, and power? For example, when considering the study of foreign languages, would it not be more relevant to the personal concerns, as well as to the current times, to offer courses in Spanish, Chinese, Russian, or an African dialect, rather than—or at least in addition to—the traditional options of Latin, French, and German?

It is Tier I that serves as the information and skills retrieval base. It is the most highly automated, individually paced, self-instructional, materials-centered tier. Most of the current discussion on individualized and programmed instruction is directed to this tier. Although such undivided attention to Tier I is discouraging in many respects, it is also encouraging: for the more efficient Tier I becomes (either through IPI[15] or other means), the more time there will be for work in Tiers II and III.

Tier II, while also highly individualized, has a different flavor. Whereas in the first tier content was fed to the child, in Tier II it is drawn forth from him in the form of whatever latent talents or abilities exist or may be discovered. It would be here that everything from learning to play the tuba, working on a research project of his own design, producing a movie, studying Swahili (if that is not included in Tier I), or writing a play would occur.

Tier II is also concerned with identifying and developing talents that are usually associated with "vocational education." Marvin Feldman, Program Officer at the Ford Foundation, makes several perti-

---

[15]IPI refers to "Individually Prescribed Instruction" and is generally associated with the materials and programs developed by Professors Glaser, Lindvall, and Bolvin of the University of Pittsburgh and used in the Oakleaf School there.

nent points that we feel help to justify the inclusion of the vocational area into Tier II:

> No effort should be spared to develop appreciation and respect for the varying talents of the individual on the part of the pupil as well as of the school system. A major objective of elementary school education should be to seek out the talent in each and show its relationship to the world of work. . . . [The school should] attempt to acquaint the student with the workings of industry and commerce, and help him match his talents to his career objective. It [also should] include an annual career-objective analysis for each student as diagnosed, discussed, predicted, and evaluated by the combined resources of man-made examinations, computer-oriented methodologies, and man- and machine-derived interpretations.[15]

Tier II, then, allows for the development of individual creativity and exploration of interests.

Tier III may be thought of as group inquiry into 1) the issues and problems of social action which are personally related to the students and 2) the exploration of self and others. Inherent in this tier are programs for developing the kinds of sample objectives noted earlier (that is, "B" or social objectives, "C" or personal development objectives and "D" or connectedness objectives).

Another level of learning to learn skills—"self- and other awaring skills"—would also be explored in Tier III. These are the skills required in recognizing and describing oneself and others multidimensionally, especially in terms of feeling states and concerns. Any skills that help develop a greater range of intensity and effectiveness of communicating emotional states; that help children to get in touch with and free the flow of inner feelings; or that encourage them to more openness, authenticity, and fuller awareness of self and others would be included here.[17]

We have seen in a number of classroom experiences that "awar-

[16]Marvin Feldman, *Making Education Relevant.* Ford Foundation pamphlet, 1966.

[17]Phrasing suggested by George I. Brown, Department of Education, University of California, Santa Barbara.

ing" skills are frequently the least developed. Often when a group of children is asked how they feel about something they have difficulty talking about it. If a child responds that he feels nervous or happy, he often has trouble telling how it feels to feel nervous or happy, much less why he feels that way or whether others feel that way too. If a child is asked to describe someone (himself included) or find out about someone, his descriptions or questions generally involve only what the person looks like, where he lives, and what he does. Seldom does he describe or question someone in terms of that person's thoughts or feelings about certain things.

In Tier III the teacher, by establishing a developmental sequence of awaring skills, can help the children elaborate self and others. Such a developmental sequence might be stated this way: Skills that facilitate—

STAGE 1. Seeing and describing what is happening to you, especially in feeling or behavior states

STAGE 2. Others seeing and describing what is happening to them

STAGE 3. Comparing, contrasting your feeling and behavior responses with those around you

STAGE 4. Analyzing the various responses and their consequences

STAGE 5. Testing alternatives—seeing how you feel when experimenting with new feelings and behaviors (for example, trying out others' feelings and behaviors)

STAGE 6. Decision-making, choice-making from feelings and behaviors you have tested out

Tier III, thus, would mainly be involved with power, identity, and connectedness and would allow for a greater emphasis on the affective *aspects* of education.

Expanding the Notion of Tier III

Since Tier III is perhaps the most unique and least familiar feature of this organization, a closer look at some of its dimensions is needed.

The Personological and
Sociological Continuum of Tier III

As previously mentioned we cannot assume because social realities, let alone social action, are introduced into a school's programming that they will automatically guarantee contact with the learner. Nor can we assume that because the children are actively involved in influencing their immediate realities, the sense of individual potency will have been achieved. The acquisition of power does not necessarily make a person feel powerful. As good evidence of this, one may view any number of political figures in our country. While they may be in very powerful positions, they often appear extremely vulnerable to criticism and are intimidated by public opinion polls. There appears to be a distinction between power *over* others through social status and role and the feelings of power within one's self.

It is because of this distinction that Tier III must consistently provide a simultaneous range of experiences from the personological (intrapersonal) to the sociological (interpersonal) domains. The issues of identity, power, and connectedness pervade both domains and everything in between them.

In the accompanying chart (see Figure 2), curricular objectives and operational means must be developed at both ends of the continuum. For example, while children are planning and carrying out an action to get heat in a tenement building (that is sociological), they should also be exploring how they see themselves in terms of weakness and strength and expanding their own criteria for self-evaluation in this category, (that is, personological). Another example of this could involve the students doing cross-age teaching of younger children. During such an activity the student would be engaged in interacting with children, while he would at the same time be exploring the child subself within himself. Thus he would be developing sensitivity to others (sociological), while also seeing more dimensions of his own self (personological).

The following is an illustration of how this looks with the use of adults in a teacher-training program at Teachers College (TC), Columbia University.

PSYCHOSOCIAL RANGE
OF
TIER III

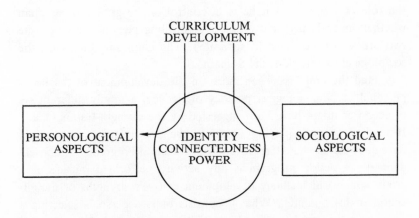

CURRICULUM
DEVELOPMENT

PERSONOLOGICAL
ASPECTS

IDENTITY
CONNECTEDNESS
POWER

SOCIOLOGICAL
ASPECTS

FIGURE 2

A "strength-training team" has been working with students in a preservice program at TC on the "climate" projected by the teachers-to-be when they walk into a classroom of children on their first day of school. Briefly, what happens is that the three members of the strength team as well as some classmates of the target person (that is, the person assuming the role of new teacher) role-play children who are giving the teacher a hard time. After 10 or 15 minutes of being in front of the role players and attempting to maintain control and establish classroom procedures, the preservice teacher is rated by the team and classmates on the general impression he made upon the "children." Kids' terms such as "flakey," "uptight," "with it," are used to evaluate the over-all performance; and the *specific* behaviors that caused the teacher to be labeled as such are explored. Certain alternative behaviors that might have been more effective and that seem to fit the personality or capitalize on the already existing strengths of the particular teacher are suggested. The teacher then practices these behaviors again in front of the role players.

Although these sessions are to the teacher, to an extent, a direct confrontation of his particular strengths and weaknesses, the emphasis is on developing his classroom management skills and on his abilities to take control of a group, rather than on a total personality revamping. The trainers are concerned with how well the trainee can act (in the role of teacher) as if he is in control of the group, rather than whether he feels personally like a controlling person (although the two are sometimes hard to separate). The emphasis thus is on the sociological or interpersonal domain.

Had the emphasis been more on the development of the intrapersonal or personological potency or agency, a totally different set of exercises might have been suggested by the strength-training team. Instead of the role-playing situation, the preservice teachers might have engaged in what Herbert Otto calls "Action Programs."[18] Loosely defined, an action program is any activity performed outside of a group which will facilitate development of one's strengths or mobilization of his potential. What it consists of is a person's selecting a series of rather easily achievable activities that he has always wanted to do but somehow has avoided doing for various reasons. Anything from planting a garden to changing a hairdo to trying a new food, visiting an art gallery, talking to a professor or the boss, and so forth, are types of activities that might be selected by an individual. The criteria for selection of the action programs are that they will do the most for *you,* are fun, contain elements of spontaneity, and have a high probability of success. The individual then keeps a chart of the progress he has made in realizing one of the goals per week.

Although this is a sketchy description of Otto's notion of action programs, it gives a flavor of what we see as an example of a more personological experience that can help develop feelings of intrapersonal strength or power within one's self. In this situation the individual has really been negotiating with the subself roles or cast of characters inside, rather than outside, of him (such as he had to do in the classroom-control episode).

The major attempt, then, in Tier III is to effect a more clinical marriage between the personal and social domains as they bear on identity, connectedness, and power. As Erikson so ably puts it "we

[18]Herbert A. Otto, *Group Methods Designed to Actualize Human Potential: A Handbook.* From the Human Potentials Research Project, University of Utah, Salt Lake City, 1967, p. 19.

cannot separate personal growth and communal change, nor can we separate . . . the identity crisis in individual life and contemporary crises in historical development because the two help to define each other and are truly relative to each other. In fact, the whole interplay between the psychological and the social, the developmental and the historical, for which identity is of prototypal significance, could be conceptualized only as a kind of psychological relativity.[19]

The Clinical Or Action Aspect of Tier III

Another dimension of Tier III concerns its clinical aspect. By clinical we mean applying behaviors to reality. We are here concerned with total behavior, not simply symbolic, and its effect on real life situations. Tier I relies on the academic and its related cognitive aspects as an intervention strategy for working with the learner, and although it may make use of real life situations, its major aim is to expand the way a person might *think* about the situation. But in Tier III, thinking becomes instrumental to the *actions* of the individual, for it is the actions that are the primary aim.

It is conceivable that some Tier I and Tier III areas might be similar, but each would have a different purpose. For example, suppose we were formulating programs on the issue of connectedness: In Tier I we might consider the use of the Lippitt and Fox social studies programs, which teach children to analyze various kinds of interactions between people, the way a social scientist would.[20] The student would use real life situations, including possibly themselves, for the purposes of concept development and the development of analytical procedures. They would be viewing the phenomena as an *objective observer*—the way a social scientist is supposed to be viewing. In a Tier III program, the learner, instead of learning to assume the role of an objective observer, would now be involved as a *subjective par-*

[19]Erik H. Erikson, *Identity, Youth and Crisis.* New York: W. W. Norton and Co., 1968, p. 23.

[20]Ronald Lippitt and Robert Fox, with the assistance of the University of Michigan Social Science Education Staff, have prepared a series of interesting social science units. The units, including student resource books and teacher handbooks, are copyrighted 1965 by Science Research Associated, Inc., Chicago, Ill.

ticipant. Instead of learning to analyze he would be learning to act—or learning to apply some of his thinking to his own behaviors as he interacts with others. He would be involved in basic encounters with others and would be learning new ways for assimilating feedback. He would now be an "insider" rather than an "outsider."

Tier III then is highly clinical and experiential, although still retaining a cognitive flavor, since we do not wish children merely to experience, but rather to utilize cognitive organizers for getting the most mileage from their experiences. What we would try to create would be a program that would achieve a more complete integration between thoughts, feelings, and actions. This brings us to a third dimension of Tier III, the feelings.

The Affective or Feeling Dimension of Tier III[21]

The one ingredient perhaps most vital to the operations of Tier III is emphasis on the affective or feeling domain of the students. Attempts must be made in Tier III for greater harmony between the affective and the cognitive functioning of the students as these apply to their actions or behavior.[22]

---

[21]For a closer look into the possibilities of the affective domain, see the Ford Foundation report *A Model for Developing a Relevant Curriculum* by Gerald Weinstein and Mario D. Fantini. In this report the authors more fully explain the role of affect and offer the beginnings of sample "pieces" of curriculum (units, lessons, diagnostic techniques) based on affect and especially on the concerns of identity, power, and connectedness.

[22]In "What Tasks for the Schools," *Saturday Review* (January 1967), p. 41, Sterling M. McMurrin, former U.S. Commissioner of Education, summarizes the definitions of cognitive and affective:

> The cognitive function of instruction is directed to the achievement and communication of knowledge, both the factual knowledge of the sciences and the formal relationships of logic and mathematics—Knowledge is both specific data and generalized structure. It is discipline in the ways of knowing, involving perception, the inductive, deductive, and intuitive processes and the techniques of analysis and generalization. It involves the immediate grasp of sensory objects and the abstractive processes by which the intellect constructs its ideas and fashions its ideals. The affective function of instruction pertains to the practical life—to the emotions, the passions, the dispositions, the motives, the moral and aesthetic sensibilities, the capacity for feeling, concern, attachment or detachment, sympathy, empathy, and appreciation.

In Tier I affect or feelings may be used as motivational devices to link the outside content to inside natural dispositions. In schools today this is usually the only way that the children's feelings are used —as tools to induce the child to get to the prescribed academic cognitive content. Cognition thus is the end product of the process. Yet, as stated in the article "Reducing the Behavior Gap":

> . . . it is obvious that knowing something cognitively does not always result in behavior that follows on that knowing. This is because knowledge alone cannot influence total behavior. Moreover, all kinds of knowledge are not equally influential. The missing ingredient in this equation seems to be knowledge that is related to the affective or emotional world of the learner.
>
> What most often prompts action or behavior is a feeling or emotion about something rather than knowledge per se. It may be that "knowing about" can prompt feeling, but it is the feeling that generates behavior. *Unless knowledge relates to feeling, it is unlikely to affect behavior appreciably.* When education begins to make better use of this basic concept, we will have taken a giant step toward reducing the behavior gap . . . [i.e., The discrepancy between much of the behavior of individuals in society and what they have been taught in school][23]

If one thinks of a school in terms of the three tiers or curricular missions one can see that each tier is not completely isolated, but instead overlaps somewhat with the others. For example, Tiers II and III would find it difficult to function completely effectively without occasionally dipping into the basic skills and information tier. Each of the three curricular modes has different strengths to offer and different weaknesses. But, blended together in proper proportions they could achieve, we feel, a far greater and more balanced educational result than can any one of them taken alone.

It is interesting to note how an organization and objectives of this kind lessen one of the great problems of the urban school—grouping. In Tiers I and II, since there is greater emphasis on individualized instruction and much less reliance on group instruction in the academic areas, individuals are not saddled with labels that are punishing. The talent and interest areas of Tier II do not require

[23]Mario D. Fantini and Gerald Weinstein, "Reducing the Behavior Gap," *NEA Journal*, vol. 57, no. 1 (January 1968), p. 24.

that everyone be at the same academic levels in order to pursue a common interest. Tier III, in which group instruction does take place, allows for heterogeneous grouping since children are not competing for grade level achievement norms. Here they are working on issues in which diverse backgrounds and experiences are *needed* to hit at problems from as many vantage points as possible. In other words, differences are required for providing the best cross-fertilization possible when dealing with social and personal concerns.

Relationship of the Three-Tiered School to Society's Demands

Perhaps it is appropriate at this point to try to make the connection between the objectives as developed in the three-tiered school and the actual product that society demands of any school. Certainly behavioral objectives imply that the learner will be doing certain things while he is in school and when he is out. But at one stage the learner will leave (will "graduate"). At that time, what must an urban school and its broadened base of relevant objectives have actually accomplished toward the major roles that society demands the graduate to play in modern life?

Certainly it is not a simple matter to project all the roles the school's product must assume. However, we can suggest four major roles that society demands and that the three-tiered school arrangement attempts to prepare students for.[24]

The Work Career

The objectives outlined must lead to the broader goal of creating educational processes that lead to careers in the "work world." Whether we emphasize basic skills in Tier I or vocational skills and interests in Tier II or social action in Tier III, each contributes to the broader role a learner must assume as wage earner. Certainly the fact

[24]A more detailed description of the four roles or careers appears in Fantini and Weinstein, *The Disadvantaged: Challenge to Education,* pp. 426–439.

that the American labor market has moved from a goods to service economy reinforces the need for urban schools to develop skills, such as those emphasized in Tier III (that is, sensitivity, empathy, human relations, positive feeling of self, and the like). Otherwise the employer will find that he must spend significant sums of money sending employees to Bethel, Maine, for "sensitivity training," or hiring special consultants in group dynamics or interpersonal relations. The point is that the work world will be demanding the very behaviors we have tried to outline in our three-tiered schools.

The "new" educational process suggested by our "model" urban school therefore is also realistic to the changing career emphases.

The Parent Career

As evidence is compiled in the behavioral sciences it becomes increasingly evident that the parent has the critical role in child growth and development. We now know that mental illness, neurosis, and psychosis can usually be traced to how well or poorly the parental role was played in the family setting.

But as important as this role of parent is, where does one learn it? What societal institution had been set up to meet this obvious need? The answer to these questions are clear. The parent learns his role when he becomes a parent, usually through trial and error.

We can no longer leave to chance the development of the role of parent. But the conventional educational process is not equipped to take over this task. As indicated earlier, the conventional school is geared to a very specific goal, subject matter mastery, and simply adding new purposes to the old process is not adequate. For example, adding one or more courses in the high school curriculum on child development or on the role of parents will probably turn out to be only an academic exercise for the students.

For our purposes the key sector of the parental role is teaching and communication. Our hypothesis is that the new educational process is itself a clinical setting for developing a more realistic parent orientation.

From the early childhood setting (for example, Operation Head

Start) to late childhood and adolescent school settings, learners at different stages can become experientially engaged in planned relationships with other children. The directors of a cross-age teaching pilot project, for example, report: "In our school pilot projects, sixth graders were involved as academic assistants in the fourth, third, second, and first grades. They helped children in the younger classrooms with reading, writing, arithmetic, spelling, and physical education. In addition, they were used as group discussion leaders and producing "behavioral specimens" presented for observation and study."[25]

The student thus is given a reality base: teaching other human beings. To illustrate, an adolescent in a three-tiered school would be assigned to an early childhood unit for certain purposes. He would begin as a teacher-aide and be given various tutorial assignments. On each assignment he should receive clinical supervision, and problems relevant to the assignment should be analyzed. In this way he would be involved in a daily interaction with others in a planned program of teaching. This activity should receive the same status, and even the same credit, as for example a course in English or history.

In addition to the actual cross-age teaching experiences built into the three-tiered school, the specific personalogical and sociological activities of Tier III are geared to the development of greater sensitivity and awareness of self and others. The general tone then of Tier III, as well as its specific activities, is designed to foster some of the very attitudes that may be most relevant to the role of parent.

If future parents perform their roles more effectively, then the growth and development problems of the past may be prevented. And if students, as future parents, have continuous experience as teachers of the young and develop sensitivity in transacting effective communications and in promoting the process of inquiry in children, a significant step will have been taken in orienting each student to the parental role.

[25]Peggy Lippitt and John E. Lohman, "Cross-Age Relationships—An Educational Resource," *Children,* vol. 12, no. 3, U.S. Department of Health, Education and Welfare, p. 115.

The Citizen Career

We have given considerable emphasis to this career in our earlier discussions of social action and participatory democracy. We have indicated that a society that aspires to continuing democratization and openness must develop citizens who perform their roles intelligently and actively. We have suggested that it is not enough for the citizen to think critically about the enormous domestic and international problems facing humanity; he must also engage in constructive social action.

The tiered school, especially Tier III, is aimed at giving the learner a direct face-to-face encounter with social injustices and alternative strategies for their resolve. Suffice it to say that the behavior objectives of the urban school envisioned by the authors will have a greater impact on the performance of the learner as an action-oriented citizen who is motivated to move toward reconstructing those injustices that negate the fullest development of the individual and the society of which he is a part.

A Career in Self-development

We have already given considerable emphasis in this book to the "self-development career," especially in our earlier discussions of the sociological and personological aspects of Tier III and of the development of individual talents and interests in Tier II.

The orientation, attitudes, concepts, and skills required to help the individual find out who he is and to enable him to continue the development of his own potential after he has left the formal educational system can be initiated early in his formal training. As we have indicated, a good part of self-development lies in the development of self-awareness and understanding that lead to a heightened awareness and empathetic understanding of others. Surely the emphasis on the more affective aspects, as seen in Tier III, is a step toward this.

In preparing pupils for a career in self-development, as well as for the three other careers, the three-tiered school does much to make the educational process congruent with its stated aims—and with the demands of society. In other words, by restructuring the curriculum to meet these four demands, a far more efficient educational process may result.

Scheduling

Probably the first reaction to the three-tiered model is, "How would you possibly do all these things within a school day?" We believe that this scheme can easily be achieved if one envisions an extended school day—with the school and numerous out-of-school instructional centers open at least 12 hours a day, six and even seven days a week. The basic organization and initiation of the studies would occur during the standard 9 A.M. to 3 P.M. schedule, but once the children are started on certain paths of study and discussion they do not have to be limited to the conventional school day. For example, as long as skills centers manned by trained skills counselors were established, students would be able to utilize these outside of the classroom for their own development in Tier I. Likewise, talent and interest centers would also be established outside the school for Tier II development. Action projects and activities related particularly to the development of a sense of power and control over situations (Tier III) would similarly take place outside of the school as well as inside. Figure 3 may help clarify some of this.

The comment at this point may be that anything can be done—any educational innovation realized—if the school day were to be lengthened. This may be true. Yet even if the school day were not extended and if instead Tier I were taught with IPI-like procedures and materials there would be more time available from 9:00 to 3:00 than there is in the present conventional scheduling, time that could be utilized for Tier II and III instruction. In addition, there already exists a movement that is gathering momentum to leave the schools open longer to allow for greater community and school involvement. Having children in the schools after 3 P.M. involved in aspects of

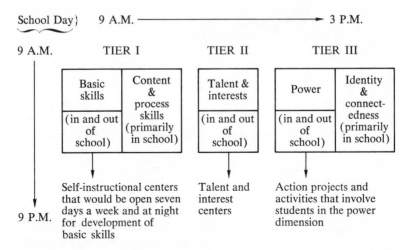

FIGURE 3

the three tiers at the same time their parents are there, perhaps engaged themselves in self-instructional labs, would do much to strengthen the relationship between school and community.

Staffing

Professional Teachers

Usually we talk about wanting good teachers for our schools, but we rarely talk about good teachers for what? We expect a single teacher to be able to effectively cover all kinds of subjects and objectives whether he is comfortable with them or not.

In the three-tiered model, however, teachers would be assigned to tiers on the basis of their strengths and interests. For example, Tier I would include technically inclined and subject-oriented teachers; Tier II would include one-to-one and activities-oriented teachers who show creativity and wide ranges of interests; Tier III would include more inductive, open-ended, child-situation-oriented teachers who would collaborate with the community on social action projects and identity training.

**Table 1   Attaching Proficiency Model
by Categories of Learning Tasks[a]**

Teacher Type and Proficiency	Learning Task Category
	Tier III
5. Facilitator of Attitude and Interpersonal Behavior Development: Human relations, attitudes, and skills	Attaining a variety of human relations attitudes and behaviors, for example, acceptance and appreciation of cultural differences, group process, group leadership roles.
	Tier II
4. Developer of Talents and Aptitudes: A skill for developing a talent	Developing a potential talent in a specialized area, for example, proficiency in dealing with higher mathematical concepts, playing a musical instrument, writing plays.
3. Identifier of Talents: Skill in promoting exploration in broad fields	Identifying interests and aptitudes appertaining to interests, for example, exploratory experiences in industrial arts, stenography, music, creative writing, earth science.
	Tier I
2. Liberal Enlightener: Skill as a master presenter	Enlightenment in the areas in which knowledge of the general population is considered important but in which every individual is not required to be proficient, for example, types of literature, geological structure, weaving rugs.
1. Teacher Technologist: Skill in administering basic skills and knowledges.	Mastering skills and knowledges considered essential for all, for example, reading, historical facts of nations, computational skills.

[a]Bernard H. McKenna, *School Staffing Patterns*. Pamphlet from the California Teachers Association, Berlingame, Calif.

A more explicit breakdown of the teacher types is made by Bernard H. McKenna in his pamphlet, *School Staffing Patterns*. Although McKenna has not designated the teacher types in terms of staffing for a three-tiered school, his delineation of them nevertheless fits nicely into that scheme (the breakdown for the three-tiers has been inserted by the authors into the original McKenna list). See Table 1. We might even modify McKenna's fifth type so that it stresses behavior more than attitudes, and break it down into two categories:

5a. Facilitator of Inter- and Intra-Personal Behaviors
5b. Facilitator of Social Action Behaviors

In addition, community people and parents would also be assigned to each of the tiers on the same basis the regular teachers would be; this leads to our next point.

Parents, Community, and Other Resource Personnel

Making urban schools work also involves tapping new resources in new ways as school personnel. We are all familiar with the work of parent associations, homeroom mothers, school volunteers, and the like. A three-tiered school provides opportunities for bringing even more kinds of diverse talents and energies into the school.

In Tier I, for example, where basic skills and academic mastery are emphasized, a systematic tutorial program can be developed. Tutoring could involve local college students on a regular basis to increase their awareness in sensitivity to urban school problems and to increase their motivation to enter careers in teaching. But perhaps more important, tutors can be *parents* who need not have a high school diploma. For example, Professor Ellson at the University of Indiana is developing an extremely promising process for training tutors to teach reading.[26] Programmed tutoring, as this process is sometimes labeled, is a device for individualizing teaching, based upon principles of programmed instruction, which can be successfully carried out by "nonprofessional" personnel with a minimum of training. Since learning to read is basic to success in almost all future activities, the idea

[26]Douglas G. Ellson, Professor of Psychology, University of Indiana, Bloomington, Ind.

of supplementing the professional teacher with aides who have been successfully taught to teach reading to five- or six-year-olds can be a tremendous asset not only to the teacher but also to the aide. Because of such a program, the aide experiences success (and thus potency), as well as being paid a respectable salary for his important effort.

Of course, the use of tutoring aides can lead to the further development of a career-ladder in which paid aides such as programmed tutors can eventually move to teacher assistants, teacher associates, and ultimately to teacher in any of the tiers. Such a career-ladder requires that community colleges and teacher-training institutions collaborate with urban schools to recognize a different set of credentialling from the standard practices now governing entry into the teaching profession.[27]

Thus, the involvement of parents in Tier I would be primarily in terms of teacher aides who are trained to work with various *academic* skill areas.

In Tier II, parents and community people who have special interests, talents, or hobbies would be tapped as talent and vocational skills identifiers and developers, thereby expanding the reservoir of resource people into a greater pool than is normally available in a single school. For example, learners whose talents are assessed in art can be matched with artists in the community; those whose talents rest with poetry and prose can be linked with poets and writers, as developed by Bud Shulberg in Watts and Herb Kohl in Harlem. The same can be accomplished with music, drama, dance, karate, or the vocational skills of car mechanics, electrical wiring, and so forth.

The community can offer rich laboratories that extend the classroom beyond the four walls of a neighborhood school. In this way, also, the problem of racial isolation can be challenged. The tiered school, for example, would not attempt to duplicate the world of work or the world of art: it could not. A more sensible way would be to take the learner to new "classrooms" with new "teachers" that is, new "clinical professors" such as a jazz musician, poet, engineer, scientist, and so on, thus contributing directly to a more natural

---

[27]For further analysis of career-ladders, see Arthur Pearl and Frank Riessman, *New Careers for the Poor*. New York: The Free Press, 1965.

and pragmatic form of integration in which all races connect with one another around common talents and interests.

In Tier III the learner can be taught by community-action specialists. These may be from the local community-action projects sponsored by the Office of Economic Opportunity (OEO) or other civil rights or community development enterprises. Moreover, other specialists in group process, basic-encounter, human relations, and the like, can be utilized from the college and university community.

The tiered school allows, as we have seen, for the "opening up" of the school as a community institution and for the flow of new energies and talents in and out of the school. In fact, the classroom at the school becomes extended to include the total community, utilizing more fully the real world of work, the community in action toward social equality, and the community as an environment for art and science. Newer disciplines can find legitimacy in such a school. Sociologists, anthropologists, engineers, systems analysts, public administrators, political strategists can all be tapped more functionally, and their entry can revitalize the total dynamic of the urban school (and vice versa, since these same resources will learn from the experience and feed these new learnings back to their respective roles; thus, an anthropologist who teaches at a city college can enrich his competence at the college level, with college students).

A Special Case
for the Teen-age Participant

One of the key socializing agents—that is, key teachers—is the adolescent. He teaches other adolescents and younger children. Some adolescents develop highly capable leadership skills that are seldom tapped to enrich the lives of themselves or their followers. We are all familiar with the so-called teen-age culture. In urban ghettos adolescents play particularly important roles. Many young children identify with older adolescent leaders and are directly influenced by them. Many of the leaders are dropouts and have taken to addiction, hustling, and the like. If they can be developed to set more positive types of examples, a valuable resource will have been tapped.

One program that has successfully worked with the adolescent and young adult mobilized as leader and teacher of younger children is the New York Urban League Street Academies program. Funded initially by the Ford Foundation and now supported by public and private money (business and industry), the program is aimed at identifying the street leaders, many of whom are dropouts. These leaders are then trained as street workers who convince other dropouts to "try again" through street academics or street corner schools. At the street academies the leaders who are "believable" begin to "tell it like it is" and make contact with other dropouts to begin the process of re-entry into school. From the Street Academy, the dropout moves to transitional academies in which he is given intensive academic briefing in order to qualify him for re-entry into prep school or into academic high schools. The ultimate aim is to convince him that he can make it—make it to college.

In other programs, as mentioned earlier, cross-age teaching is utilized in which older children are taught to be teachers of younger children in different fields. The documented results in most cases indicate a positive effect on both the older and younger learner.

In a tiered school, since the tiers offer far more than just one area for making a legitimate contribution, the opportunities for tapping more of the teen-ager's energies are enhanced. The crucial point is that the adolescent as teacher is given a new sense of purpose, dignity, and potency while influencing positively the lives of his peers and younger colleagues. Needless to say, if the teen-ager is not tapped, there is much evidence that his frustration and energies may be manifested increasingly in destructive ways.

A Word about Teacher Training

As presently practiced, teacher education differentiates its programs in two basic ways:

1. Age of child to be taught—early childhood, elementary or secondary
2. and Subject specialty—science, language, social studies, and so forth.

Preparing teachers for a three-tiered school would involve a much greater degree of differentiated training than is currently available. And this applies to key roles as well as supportive roles.

Since a great deal must be done in clarifying the curriculum of the three-tiered school, as well as the roles needed to implement that curriculum, we cannot talk very rationally about how teachers would be trained. Right now, however, it looks as though Tier III and Tier II may require the most radical departure from present training programs.

The basic question that must be answered in preparing teachers for an urban school is: Should we continue preparing them for a school that does not work or for one that will work? The answer is obvious. We cannot continue to prepare teachers to fit into an outmoded system. Rather, teacher training should be oriented toward (1) a new system such as the three-tired school, and (2) ways of dealing with community dynamics.

RELATIONSHIP
OF THE SCHOOL
TO THE COMMUNITY

Although this topic may seem at first peripheral to the explanation and development of a three-tiered school per se, one can scarcely talk of *any* type of school for an urban area without further examining its relationship to the community, for it is the community that ultimately determines whether the school will work.

As previously implied, public schools in American society belong to the public. In large urban areas the highly bureaucratized school organization has become unresponsive to the needs and aspirations of the publics within its diverse communities. A new and more dynamic relationship has to be cultivated between parents, other community people, and the urban schools. Schools need to be viewed as "open" institutions that serve *people* not just children.

A Community School Serving People

The major thrust of our presentation has been with making urban schools more relevant for children. However, we can hardly ignore the notion that for urban schools to work they must also serve adults. Consequently we can consider the community-centered aspects of a school as a "fourth tier."

The movement toward so-called community schools is only now beginning. Many urban school programs that began by focusing on the "deprived child" have gradually expanded the normal daytime programs into the afternoon and evening; after-school programs for children now extend into evening programs for parents. Drama, clubs; child care training; literacy classes; courses in basic skills and vocational skills, in parliamentary procedure; and similar projects soon take form and shape. Before long the school may be open seven days a week from early morning to late evening, offering a variety of programs for all ages.

In Flint, Michigan, for example, each of the 54 schools in the district is a Community School and is so named. A Community School Director is assigned to each community school and is responsible for coordinating its afternoon and evening programs. A varied program of education, recreation, and cultural enrichment is scheduled. The community itself has requested such clubs as a senior citizens', bridge, women's, men's, and athletic. In addition, the Mott Foundation Program of the Flint Board of Education offers day and evening programs for parents and children from "sunrise singers" each morning and roller skating in the afternoon, to ceramics in the evening.

Community Schools serve more than a social, recreational, or strictly academic function, however. Parents can use the school to discuss and plan civic programs. Community schools can serve as forums for solving a variety of community problems such as school integration, urban renewal, family relocation, and organization of indigenous neighborhood leadership. Daytime students could be involved in any of these evening seminars as a phase of the citizen career orientation which emphasized participatory behaviors.

In New Haven, Community Schools are defined as:

1. An educational center—as the place where children and adults have opportunities for study and learning
2. A center for community services—as the place where individuals may obtain health services, counseling services, legal aid, employment services, and the like

3. An important center of neighborhood and community life—as an institutional agency that will assist citizens in the study and solution of significant neighborhood problems.

A more detailed articulation of a community school was made by Leonard Covello who pioneered the concept of a community-centered school in New York City with a predominantly Italian community:

> It would seem, therefore, that the broad principles of the community-centered school might be conceptualized as the utilization of the school—
> 1.   as explorer of community social backgrounds, as a research agency, and as the medium for the practical application of the knowledge acquired through these means to the school-community program;
> 2.   as coordinator—through the school curriculum—of school departments, personnel, extra curricular activities, and so forth, with the activities of students and the community;
> 3.   as planner—through continuous curriculum revision—for the actual needs of the child within the community patterns and interests;
> 4.   as a direct channel of inter-communication between school and community, through contacts with homes, youth groups, community social agencies, and the broader phases of community life;
> 5.   as a participant, through social committees composed of students, teachers, parents, and community representatives of all the groups, in community activities, as educational media for students and community residents;
> 6.   as instigator of community participation in the conduct of the school and in the use of the school's resources;
> 7.   as a base for the establishment of "outposts" in the community; *i.e.* units of experiment in solving community problems;
> 8.   as a socializing agency in intercultural relationships and the expansion of the local social world; in the development of community-consciousness and communal cooperative effort;
> 9.   as a center for adult education in relation to objectively evaluated community needs;
> 10.   as an educational guidance center, mainly for pupils, but also for adults and community groups, and for leisure time activities;
> 11.   as a testing ground for leadership ability within the school, and for training community leadership.[28]

[28]Leonard Covello, *The Social Background of the Italo-American School Child*. Leiden, The Netherlands: E. J. Brill, 1967, pp. 414–415.

Whether each school can be a center that attempts to coordinate such a wide range of human services for people is dependent on many factors (money, personnel, space, and so forth). Our point is that certain key schools—perhaps an intermediate school that services a distinct geographical neighborhood, including "feeder" elementary schools—can serve this function initially.

The urban school as a center for adult activity can help restore a new sense of connection of the adult to the school. Moreover, the community-oriented school can become a social institution helping people to retain their sense of *cultural* identity while they search for ways of connecting to each of the other diverse *groups* that make up the human community.

Today the black community especially is making its move to regain, retain, and perpetuate its own rich culture. A school responsive to the unique style of the black (the same could be said for the Puerto Rican, Chinese, etc.) community would develop programs that enhance the cultural traditions of black people through art, music, language, festivals, memorials, and the like.

Presently many minorities are beginning to realize that urban schools not only are insensitive to their culture, but actually force both the child and adult to "give up" his culture in such a way that he ends up giving up his identity. With black people who have faced discrimination as a way of life, this realization that the school has failed them in so many ways leads to increased frustration, which in turn leads to forms of withdrawal or retaliation. Urban schools must wake up to the fact that pluralism is not only a basic tenet of an open society, but that it is moreover a necessary force for self-renewal, serving also as a mediator against the pressure of conformity that characterizes our mass technological age.

Schools responsive to the needs, aspirations, and cultural style of the communities they serve stand a greater chance of harnessing the energies of professionals, students, parents, and community residents in building a more viable urban social institution.

Community Control and Urban Schools

We have indicated that direct participation in the educational process is basic to the success of a tiered school. However, participation as we have described it in the form of a "fourth tier" as well as in the involvement of parents and community people staffing all the tiers, is one thing; determining who governs the urban school is quite another.

We have said that the failure of the schools to serve urban clients has resulted in a reassessment of the relationship of the clients (that is, students, parents, and community) to the schools and to those who run them. We are experiencing the results of this estrangement in many of our urban centers. In New York City, for example, IS 201 has become a symbol for a new movement toward greater community voice in determining educational policy. The movement is spreading to other cities. Community residents are raising demands ranging from greater voice to complete control. Urban communities are at different stages on this continuum, but what appears clear is that the issue on either end of the continuum is community control. The community residents are demanding a greater voice and control, not as a privilege but as a *right*.

Further, high school students are beginning to develop their own demands concerning what needs to happen to make urban school more relevant. In Philadelphia nearly 4000 students marched on the Board of Estimate with a list of demands. Demands from students range from better food in cafeterias to the inclusion of Swahili in the curriculum.

Consequently there are emerging "new" legitimate publics that want to stand side by side with teachers, administrators, central boards, and so on, in deciding what happens next to urban schools. Change introduced and proposed by any one public stands the chance of being vetoed by others.

While these are the interested parties that make up urban public education, they are now on a journey of disconnection well outlined in the "Bundy Report," *Reconnection for Learning: A Community School System for New York City*.[29] Unless the energies which these parties generate are harnessed around a common purpose—school reform, making schools work—then these same energies will be used in battling one another at the expense of each other and, of course, of the learner.

[29]*Reconnection for Learning: A Community School System for New York City.* Report of the Mayor's Advisory Panel on Decentralization of the New York City Schools, New York, 1967.

Perhaps one way to harness some of these energies is through a school-community council in which parents and community representatives along with certain professional educators would become the trustees of the school. Perhaps clusters of schools (for example a secondary school and its feeder schools) can be organized with representative governing boards to oversee the cluster. Such an arrangement would not only help connect urban communities to the schools that serve them, but would also increase the stake in developing relevant educational programs and give learners in those schools a sense of pride through identification. Moreover, the people of such a community would be given a sense of potency over a major institution that shapes their lives and the lives of their children.

As seen in the "Bundy Report" which addresses itself to the present disconnection between the school and parents and students, and which proposes a reconnection for learning through increased parent and community participation in local school policy, urban schools—three tiered or otherwise—must establish new relationships with the community. It is the *combination,* moreover, of both the three-tiered model *and* increased community participation and control that, to us, would seem to deal most directly with the social realities and needs of urban schools and their clientele.

Processes for Establishing a Tiered Urban School

The basic question becomes: In the face of the communities' growing concern for control, how is a new idea such as the tiered school implemented? The problem becomes one of *process.* In other words, while we cannot give a step-by-step plan for putting the idea into action, there are several ways in which the idea can *evolve*—in which vehicles can be created for moving toward it.

Presently urban schools tend to be controlled by professionals, as Marilyn Gittell outlines in her book *Participants and Participation.*[30] Since this is currently the situation, one process for getting a tiered

[30]Marilyn Gittell, *Participants and Participation.* New York: Frederick A. Praeger, 1966.

school going is for the professionals to introduce the idea by forming a committee composed largely of professionals who would then set up an experimental school to try out the idea.

The problem under this process is that teachers and administrators must accept the idea and be willing to engage in fundamental changes in organization and behavior. Even if resistance did not come from teachers and administrators themselves, it would come from parents and community, whose awareness of the massive failure in student performance has resulted in alienation. To them it would appear that this professional move is just another experiment on their children (for example, "Why experiment on us?" or "Why should our school be different from the best ones in the suburbs?"). Since the parents and community have not been integrally involved, they may come to see certain tiers as "frill" and to feel that a good school should be more traditional. Such perceptions point out the need for greater understanding on the part of parents and community to what quality education is all about. However, a more basic reason that certain parents and communities will raise objections is because this new idea is being *imposed* on them—it has been thrust upon them without their involvement or approval. Once again something is being done *to* them and *for* them, not *with* them or *by* them. Increasingly, communities are becoming the new gatekeepers for the schools, and innovation will be even more difficult to implement without community support and involvement.

Even if the community were silent and the professionals could move quickly to implement the idea, the question of denying parents and communities an opportunity to join the reform process should be considered. For to approach the implementation of an idea using this professional committee process would be a basic denial of the very goals of the three-tiered school in terms of power, identity, and connectedness.

The second alternative process is for the professionals to consult the community on the new idea and to seek their approval. With certain communities this pattern will also be unacceptable because the role of the residents is consultatory or advisory only. Thus the community will perceive its role as a "junior" member and feel that, once consulted, it will then be left out.

In more communities, however, the consultation and advisory status would be acceptable, for it represents a step in recognizing that parents and communities are legitimate and should be consulted, especially if the consultation role is institutionalized (that is, built into the proposed idea as an ongoing function). Thus, if this process is selected, there is a need to develop organizational vehicles for planning and carrying it out. For example, a community school advisory council or committee could be formed around the school or schools that are being considered for the experiment. Residents could develop procedures for determining representation on the advisory council as would teachers, administrators, and other interested groups. Such a body would oversee the facilitation of the plan and seek to develop the participation and involvement of the community in the undertaking.

A third alternative is for the community and professionals to develop a relationship similar to, but different from, the one suggested by the second alternative. That is, rather than the community being in a consulting position, the community and the professionals would develop a more dynamic relationship in which each is a joint or equal partner in the planning and development of a more viable school process.

The fourth alternative is to develop a process by which the community itself develops the plan and asks the professionals to join them in its translation. There are some communities that have reached a stage in which they can govern their own school and form a new trusteeship with one school or a clustering of schools. In such communities it will be the professionals who must be convinced that the process will lead to a more dynamic partnership for reform.

Communities that have reached the stage of community control are searching for new models that will make the urban school work. Urban communities that have developed local "governing boards" or "councils" as in New York City, Washington, D.C., and Boston are raising the question, After we get control, what will be our program? Whether it is a three-tiered program or other program though, the basic decision will be theirs. However, in our urban centers these communities have also experienced the most frustration with schoolmen and are likely to be the most estranged. Therefore, it is likely that these communities will seek the assistance of individuals (some in universities) whom they trust and respect.

Consequently this process will necessitate a sensitivity on the part of the professional which is difficult to visualize. The professional has been oriented to the notion that there is a body of expertise which differentiates the professional from the layman and that these lines must be kept delineated. A process in which the community takes the lead would be difficult for the professional to accept. Yet in many ways the realignment of communities that are re-establishing their *right* to make the schools more responsive to their needs offers the professional the best ally for real reform. Teachers especially (who, as victims of the present structure, are also searching for a more relevant program) should find an alliance with such communities fruitful. The unfortunate part is that the process must begin with a rather uneasy coalition between community and professionals. If both parties can manage the period of transition, the results could be most dramatic.

In all probability the second process will be most palatable to the professional who still holds the keys to most of the new urban school patterns. However, if solutions to urban school problems are not found soon, the communities will opt for the third alternative, thereby posing serious problems for the professional and requiring a basic readjustment of our entire legal structure governing the operation of big city schools.

The move toward decentralization—or community control of sections of the big city system—is increasing. New York City, Philadelphia, Newark, Louisville, Washington, and Chicago, are all considering various proposals on this theme.

The governance of schools, that is, returning the public schools to the public, is only one aspect of making urban schools work. The other is the education program itself. Increasingly, the two are converging. Both are necessary to reform. How one leads to the other will in many ways be our biggest challenge.

Perhaps it is fitting to close with the observation that when community residents—most of whom feel powerless—are given a role in which they must exercise authority and responsibility over one of the nation's major social institutions, that very role may help restore in them a sense of potency and identity. Giving the powerless a stake in restructuring urban schools can create a new environment of hope and trust for both adults and their children. What, indeed, is our alternative?

CONCLUSION

A school program involving community participation and control and arranged in three-tiered fashion would be geared to meeting the common needs of all children and adults without sacrificing individuality or cultural diversity. Moreover, it would foster the kind of meaningful mental framework that is conducive to the learning of academic subject matter; and because this learning would be personally meaningful to the pupils, the ability to transfer ideas and principles acquired in one context to another context would be engendered in the school's products. In other words, by dividing the school schedule into such segments as these three, rather than according to subject-matter learning per se, the educational process would be significantly more efficient not only in dealing with social realities but also in accomplishing its long expressed aims. Indeed, only through such reorganization and reorientation can educators hope to meet America's need for the human resources that will revitalize and perpetuate the country as a healthy and self-renewing nation.

This time of national crisis is a time for new leadership and a time when needed and effective changes in our social institutions have the best chances of being implemented and sustained. The crisis of the disadvantaged has provided educators and parents with a unique and epoch-making opportunity for effecting true and penetrating reform. What will they do with this opportunity? Will they use it to perpetuate the unwieldy, ineffective, and deteriorating status quo? Will they adopt a policy of "wait and see," reacting only after the fact to societal demands? Or will they seize this opportunity to assume the roles of initiators, revising education to become the instrument of societal reconstruction and renewal, of individual and societal health, and of human progress?

By making urban schools work we will be taking a step toward making this nation work.